V&A

DIARY 2009

F
FRANCES LINCOLN LIMITED
PUBLISHERS

Frances Lincoln Limited
4 Torriano Mews
Torriano Avenue
London NW5 2RZ
www.franceslincoln.com

The V&A Diary 2009
Copyright © Frances Lincoln Limited 2008
Text and photographs copyright
© Victoria and Albert Museum, London
Licensed by V&A Enterprises Limited

Royalties from sales of this product are covenanted to the Victoria and Albert Museum

Every effort has been made to seek permission to reproduce those images whose copyright does not reside with the V&A, and we are grateful to the individuals and the institutions that have assisted in this task. Any omissions are entirely unintentional and the details should be addressed to V&A Enterprises Limited, V&A Museum, Cromwell Road, South Kensington, London SW7 2RL

Astronomical information © Crown Copyright. Reproduced by permission of the Controller of Her Majesty's Stationery Office and the UK Hydrographic Office (www.ukho.gov.uk)

All rights reserved. No part of this publication may be reproduced, stored in a retrieval system or transmitted, in any form, or by any means, electronic, mechanical, photocopying, recording or otherwise, without either prior permission in writing from the publishers or a licence permitting restricted copying. In the United Kingdom such licences are issued by the Copyright Licensing Agency, Saffron House, 6–10 Kirby Street, London EC1N 8TS

British Library cataloguing-in-publication data
A catalogue record for this book is available from the British Library

ISBN: 978-0-7112-2836-8

Printed in China

First Frances Lincoln edition 2008

COVER: Detail of a tiara in the form of a wreath. Brilliant- and rose-cut diamonds, pearls, set in silver backed with gold. England, about 1850. Cory Bequest

BACK COVER: Photograph by John French. Outfit designed by Digby Morton. England, Autumn 1959

TITLE PAGE: Photograph by John French for *Vanity Fair*. England, July 1951

INTRODUCTION: Locket. Enamelled gold, set with table-cut diamonds, rubies and miniature painting. Czech Republic, probably Prague, about 1610–20

VISITORS' INFORMATION
The Victoria and Albert Museum
Cromwell Road
South Kensington, London SW7 2RL
Telephone: 020 7942 2000

Museum hours of opening:
10.00 to 17.45 daily
10.00 to 22.00 Fridays (selected galleries remain open after 18.00)
Closed: Christmas Eve, Christmas Day and Boxing Day

For information on the V&A Museum, please visit the website at www.vam.ac.uk. For information on V&A inspired products, please visit the V&A Shop website at www.vandashop.co.uk

For information on V&A Membership, please contact the Members' Office on 020 7942 2271

FORTHCOMING EXHIBITIONS
(Exhibition dates are subject to change so please check before making a special journey)
Cold War Modern: Art & Design in a Divided World 1945–75 (27 Sep '08–11 Jan '09)
Universal Everything (Nov '08–Jan '09)
Magnificence of the Tsars (9 Dec '08–29 Mar '09)
Bjork (13 Jan–26 April '09)
International Baroque (4 Apr–19 Jul '09)
Stephen Jones Hats (Apr '09–Jan '10)
Polish Posters (May–Nov '09)
Telling Tales (Jun–Oct '09)
Maharajas (10 Oct '09–17 Jan '10)
Digital Responses (Nov '09–Feb '10)

CALENDAR 2009

JANUARY
M T W T F S S
         1 2 3 4
5 6 7 8 9 10 11
12 13 14 15 16 17 18
19 20 21 22 23 24 25
26 27 28 29 30 31

FEBRUARY
M T W T F S S
                1
2 3 4 5 6 7 8
9 10 11 12 13 14 15
16 17 18 19 20 21 22
23 24 25 26 27 28

MARCH
M T W T F S S
                1
2 3 4 5 6 7 8
9 10 11 12 13 14 15
16 17 18 19 20 21 22
23 24 25 26 27 28 29
30 31

APRIL
M T W T F S S
      1 2 3 4 5
6 7 8 9 10 11 12
13 14 15 16 17 18 19
20 21 22 23 24 25 26
27 28 29 30

MAY
M T W T F S S
            1 2 3
4 5 6 7 8 9 10
11 12 13 14 15 16 17
18 19 20 21 22 23 24
25 26 27 28 29 30 31

JUNE
M T W T F S S
1 2 3 4 5 6 7
8 9 10 11 12 13 14
15 16 17 18 19 20 21
22 23 24 25 26 27 28
29 30

JULY
M T W T F S S
      1 2 3 4 5
6 7 8 9 10 11 12
13 14 15 16 17 18 19
20 21 22 23 24 25 26
27 28 29 30 31

AUGUST
M T W T F S S
                1 2
3 4 5 6 7 8 9
10 11 12 13 14 15 16
17 18 19 20 21 22 23
24 25 26 27 28 29 30
31

SEPTEMBER
M T W T F S S
    1 2 3 4 5 6
7 8 9 10 11 12 13
14 15 16 17 18 19 20
21 22 23 24 25 26 27
28 29 30

OCTOBER
M T W T F S S
         1 2 3 4
5 6 7 8 9 10 11
12 13 14 15 16 17 18
19 20 21 22 23 24 25
26 27 28 29 30 31

NOVEMBER
M T W T F S S
                1
2 3 4 5 6 7 8
9 10 11 12 13 14 15
16 17 18 19 20 21 22
23 24 25 26 27 28 29
30

DECEMBER
M T W T F S S
    1 2 3 4 5 6
7 8 9 10 11 12 13
14 15 16 17 18 19 20
21 22 23 24 25 26 27
28 29 30 31

CALENDAR 2010

JANUARY
M T W T F S S
              1 2 3
4 5 6 7 8 9 10
11 12 13 14 15 16 17
18 19 20 21 22 23 24
25 26 27 28 29 30 31

FEBRUARY
M T W T F S S
1 2 3 4 5 6 7
8 9 10 11 12 13 14
15 16 17 18 19 20 21
22 23 24 25 26 27 28

MARCH
M T W T F S S
1 2 3 4 5 6 7
8 9 10 11 12 13 14
15 16 17 18 19 20 21
22 23 24 25 26 27 28
29 30 31

APRIL
M T W T F S S
         1 2 3 4
5 6 7 8 9 10 11
12 13 14 15 16 17 18
19 20 21 22 23 24 25
26 27 28 29 30

MAY
M T W T F S S
                1 2
3 4 5 6 7 8 9
10 11 12 13 14 15 16
17 18 19 20 21 22 23
24 25 26 27 28 29 30
31

JUNE
M T W T F S S
   1 2 3 4 5 6
7 8 9 10 11 12 13
14 15 16 17 18 19 20
21 22 23 24 25 26 27
28 29 30

JULY
M T W T F S S
         1 2 3 4
5 6 7 8 9 10 11
12 13 14 15 16 17 18
19 20 21 22 23 24 25
26 27 28 29 30 31

AUGUST
M T W T F S S
                1
2 3 4 5 6 7 8
9 10 11 12 13 14 15
16 17 18 19 20 21 22
23 24 25 26 27 28 29
30 31

SEPTEMBER
M T W T F S S
      1 2 3 4 5
6 7 8 9 10 11 12
13 14 15 16 17 18 19
20 21 22 23 24 25 26
27 28 29 30

OCTOBER
M T W T F S S
            1 2 3
4 5 6 7 8 9 10
11 12 13 14 15 16 17
18 19 20 21 22 23 24
25 26 27 28 29 30 31

NOVEMBER
M T W T F S S
1 2 3 4 5 6 7
8 9 10 11 12 13 14
15 16 17 18 19 20 21
22 23 24 25 26 27 28
29 30

DECEMBER
M T W T F S S
      1 2 3 4 5
6 7 8 9 10 11 12
13 14 15 16 17 18 19
20 21 22 23 24 25 26
27 28 29 30 31

Introduction

'Your peacock is finished' wrote C. R. Ashbee, the architect and designer, to his wife Janet in 1900. 'He is at the present moment pinned on my coat and is preening his tail'. Illustrated on week 14 of this diary, he now preens himself in the V&A's new Jewellery Gallery, which, thanks to the vision and generosity of William and Judith Bollinger, opened in 2008. The peacock brooch is one of 3500 jewels in the gallery which continue the line from the first French and Irish jewellery bought for the Museum from the Great Exhibition in 1851.

The power of jewels lies in their beauty and their ability to embody the deepest human emotions. Jewels are a potent link with the past, a celebration of art and craftsmanship, as well as a declaration of love and loss, of faith and hope, of status and fashion. The story of jewels is the story of people, of those who made jewellery and gave it, of those who wore it and collected it.

Sometimes we know the names of the makers and owners of the jewels illustrated. A pendant enclosing a miniature by Nicholas Hilliard was given by Elizabeth I to her Vice-Chamberlain, Thomas Heneage. A gold box by Ricart with a cameo by Garelli was given by Napoleon to his sister, Caroline, Queen of Naples. Research in Russia has shown that a group of 46 diamond dress ornaments was commissioned by Catherine the Great from Leopold Pfisterer in 1764. Later they were worn by Grand Duke Mikhail Alexandrovich, killed like his brother, Nicholas II, in 1918.

Sometimes names are lacking, but the purpose of the jewel is clear. A woman in Ancient Egypt wore a pendant of the hippopotamus goddess Taweret to give her good fortune in childbirth. A lover in about 1400 gave a heart brooch with the engraved declaration 'ourselves and all things at your desire'. A woman in the sixteenth century wore a pendant with hessonite garnet and peridot to protect her through the properties of the stones and the invocations inscribed on the reverse.

Many collectors, or owners of a single jewel, have generously seen the V&A as a home in which their jewellery would be widely appreciated. Chauncey Hare Townshend bequeathed a collection of specimen gemstones mounted in rings. Dame Joan Evans, a pre-eminent jewellery historian, gave over 600 jewels, including the heart brooch. Lady Cory, a dedicated needlewoman married to a coal and oil magnate, gave Catherine the Great's diamonds and much else. More recently Patricia V. Goldstein, a redoubtable New York dealer and collector, has given through the American Friends of the V&A an extensive collection of jewels by European and American jewellery houses in thanks for her visits to the jewellery gallery 'where I would wander for an hour or two in blissful serenity'.

Richard Edgcumbe
Sculpture, Metalwork, Ceramics and Glass Department

DECEMBER · JANUARY

29 Monday

30 Tuesday

31 Wednesday — New Year's Eve

1 Thursday — New Year's Day
Holiday, UK, Republic of Ireland, Canada,
USA, Australia and New Zealand

WEEK 1

2 Friday   Holiday, Scotland and New Zealand

3 Saturday

4 Sunday   First Quarter

Pair of earrings. Turquoise and gold, with rose- and brilliant-cut diamonds. Britain, 1850–60. Cory Bequest

January

WEEK 2

5 Monday

6 Tuesday — Epiphany

7 Wednesday

8 Thursday

9 Friday

10 Saturday

11 Sunday — *Full Moon*

Advertisement from *La Femme Chic* magazine. France, 1948

January

12 Monday

13 Tuesday

14 Wednesday

15 Thursday

WEEK 3

16 Friday

17 Saturday

18 Sunday
Last Quarter

Pendant with cameo portrait of Marie de Medici. Made by Carlo Giuliano (about 1831–95), cameo by Georges Bissinger. Enamelled gold, set with sardonyx (layered agate) cameo, rubies, sapphires, rock crystal and pearls. England, London, about 1865. Given by Carlo and Arthur Giuliano

JANUARY

WEEK 4

19 Monday Holiday, USA (Martin Luther King's Birthday)

20 Tuesday

21 Wednesday

22 Thursday

23 Friday

24 Saturday

25 Sunday

Two bow ornaments. Brilliant-cut diamonds set in silver. Russia, about 1760. Cory Bequest

January · February

WEEK 5

26 Monday

New Moon
Chinese New Year
Holiday, Australia (Australia Day)

27 Tuesday

28 Wednesday

29 Thursday

30 Friday

31 Saturday

1 Sunday

Photograph by John French. Outfit designed by Digby Morton. England, Autumn 1959

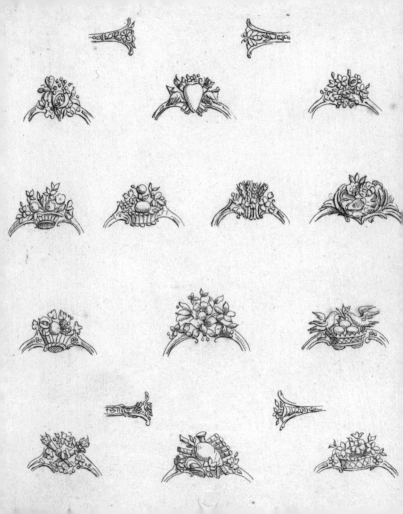

February

WEEK 6

2 Monday

First Quarter

3 Tuesday

4 Wednesday

5 Thursday

6 Friday

Holiday, New Zealand (Waitangi Day)
Accession of Queen Elizabeth II

7 Saturday

8 Sunday

Traité des pierres précieuses et de la manière de les employer en parure. Plates engraved by Mlle Raimbau after original design by J.B Piauger. Published in France, Paris, 1762

FEBRUARY

9 Monday *Full Moon*

10 Tuesday

11 Wednesday

12 Thursday Holiday, USA (Lincoln's Birthday)

WEEK 7

13 Friday

14 Saturday   St. Valentine's Day

15 Sunday

Brooch. Gold, engraved, formerly enamelled, inscribed on the reverse in French 'Ourselves and all things at your whim'. England or France. About 1400

FEBRUARY

WEEK 8

16 Monday
Last Quarter
Holiday, USA (Washington's Birthday)

17 Tuesday

18 Wednesday

19 Thursday

20 Friday

21 Saturday

22 Sunday

Advertisement from *La Femme Chic* magazine. France, 1948

FEBRUARY · MARCH

23 Monday

24 Tuesday
Shrove Tuesday

25 Wednesday
New Moon
Ash Wednesday

26 Thursday

WEEK 9

27 Friday

28 Saturday

1 Sunday St David's Day

Rings. Britain, about 1850. Townshend collection
Top left: Bi-colour yellow/orange topaz set in gold
Top right: Orange topaz set in gold
Bottom: Orange sapphire set in gold

MARCH

WEEK 10

2 Monday

3 Tuesday

4 Wednesday

First Quarter

5 Thursday

6 Friday

7 Saturday

8 Sunday

Photograph by John French. Day dress, Cotton Board, England, 1956

March

9 Monday   Commonwealth Day

10 Tuesday

11 Wednesday   Full Moon

12 Thursday

13 Friday

14 Saturday

15 Sunday

Left: Design for a necklace, by Arthur Gaskin (1862–1928) and Georgie Gaskin (1868–1934). Pencil, chalk, water- and body-colour. England, 1910

Right: 'Love in a Mist' Necklace. Made by Georgie Cave Gaskin (1868–1934). Silver, enamel and pearls. England, Olton (Warwickshire), about 1910. Given by Mrs. Emmeline H. Cadbury

MARCH

WEEK 12

16 Monday

17 Tuesday
St. Patrick's Day
Holiday, Northern Ireland and Republic of Ireland

18 Wednesday
Last Quarter

19 Thursday

20 Friday
Vernal Equinox

21 Saturday

22 Sunday
Mothering Sunday, UK

Advertisement from *La Femme Chic* magazine, France, 1948

March

WEEK 13

23 Monday

24 Tuesday

25 Wednesday

26 Thursday   *New Moon*

27 Friday

28 Saturday

29 Sunday   British Summer Time begins

Necklace with pendant mask of the river god Achelous. Made by Carlo Giuliano (about 1831–95). Granulated gold. Britain, about 1865

MARCH · APRIL

30 Monday

31 Tuesday

1 Wednesday

2 Thursday					First Quarter

WEEK 14

3 Friday

4 Saturday

5 Sunday Palm Sunday

Left: Design for a gold necklace set with pearls, with a pendant in the form of a peacock. Made by Charles Robert Ashbee (1863–1942). Pencil and watercolour. England, May 1905

Right: Pendant-brooch in the form of a peacock. Designed by Charles Robert Ashbee (1863–1942) and made by Adolf Gebardt at the Guild of Handicraft, Essex House, London. Silver and gold set with blister pearls, garnet and brilliant-cut diamonds. England, London, 1900

April

WEEK 15

6 Monday

7 Tuesday

8 Wednesday

9 Thursday

Full Moon
Maundy Thursday
Passover (Pesach), First Day

10 Friday

Good Friday
Holiday, UK, Canada, USA, Australia and New Zealand

11 Saturday

12 Sunday

Easter Day

Design for a jewelled cross, by Reinhold Vasters (1827–1909). Pencil, pen and ink, and watercolour. Germany, about 1850–1900

April

13 Monday

Easter Monday
Holiday, UK (exc. Scotland), Republic of Ireland, Canada,
Australia and New Zealand

14 Tuesday

15 Wednesday

Passover (Pesach), Seventh Day

16 Thursday

Passover (Pesach), Eighth Day

WEEK 16

17 Friday
Last Quarter

18 Saturday

19 Sunday

Ring. Quartz citrine set in gold. Townshend Collection

April

WEEK 17

20 Monday

21 Tuesday
Birthday of Queen Elizabeth II

22 Wednesday

23 Thursday
St. George's Day

24 Friday

25 Saturday
New Moon
Holiday, Australia and New Zealand (Anzac Day)

26 Sunday

Detail of a tiara in the form of a wreath. Brilliant- and rose-cut diamonds, pearls, set in silver backed with gold. England, about 1850. Cory Bequest

April · May

27 Monday

28 Tuesday

29 Wednesday

30 Thursday

WEEK 18

1 Friday *First Quarter*

2 Saturday

3 Sunday

Prophylatic pendant. Enamelled gold, hessonite garnet, peridot and sapphire drop. Inscribed at the back 'ANNANISAPTA + DEI' (against epilepsy) and 'DETRAGRAMMATA IHS MARIA'. England, about 1540–60

May

WEEK 19

4 Monday   Early Spring Bank Holiday, UK and Republic of Ireland

5 Tuesday

6 Wednesday

7 Thursday

8 Friday

9 Saturday   *Full Moon*

10 Sunday   Mother's Day, USA, Canada, Australia and New Zealand

Photograph by John French, for Rembrandt Booklet. England, 1963

May

11 Monday

12 Tuesday

13 Wednesday

14 Thursday

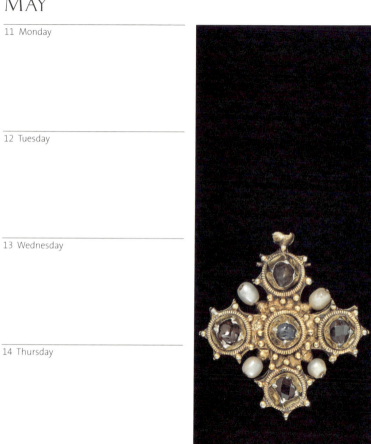

WEEK 20

15 Friday

16 Saturday

17 Sunday — *Last Quarter*

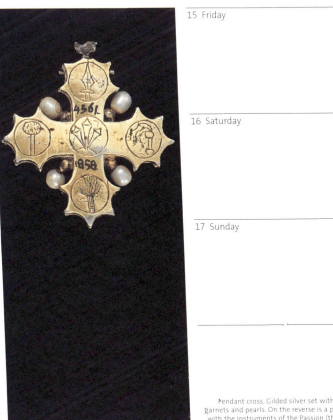

Pendant cross. Gilded silver set with ruby, sapphire, garnets and pearls. On the reverse is a plaque engraved with the Instruments of the Passion (the last events in Christ's earthly life). Possibly Germany, 1400–1500

May

WEEK 21

18 Monday

Holiday, Canada (Victoria Day)

19 Tuesday

20 Wednesday

21 Thursday

Ascension Day

22 Friday

23 Saturday

24 Sunday

New Moon

Bangle. Made by Verger Fréres for Chaumet. Gold set with rubies, brilliant-cut diamonds set in platinum. France, Paris, 1935–45. Given by the American Friends of the V&A through the generosity of Patricia V. Goldstein

MAY

WEEK 22

25 Monday — Spring Bank Holiday, UK / Holiday, USA (Memorial Day)

26 Tuesday

27 Wednesday

28 Thursday

29 Friday — Feast of Weeks (Shavuot)

30 Saturday

31 Sunday — *First Quarter* / Whit Sunday (Pentecost)

Necklace. Made by Alexander Calder (1898–1976) Brass wire. France, Paris, about 1938

June

1 Monday — Holiday, Republic of Ireland
Holiday, New Zealand (Queen's Birthday)

2 Tuesday — Coronation Day

3 Wednesday

4 Thursday

WEEK 23

5 Friday

6 Saturday

7 Sunday *Full Moon*
Trinity Sunday

Brooch. Designed by Bernard Instone (1891–1987). Silver, enamel and pearls. England, Birmingham, 1940–50

June

WEEK 24

8 Monday

9 Tuesday

10 Wednesday

11 Thursday

Corpus Christi

12 Friday

13 Saturday

The Queen's Official Birthday

14 Sunday

Photograph by John French of Jean Shrimpton modelling jewellery, *Voice & Vision*. England, May 1963

June

15 Monday — Last Quarter / St. Swithin's Day

16 Tuesday

17 Wednesday

18 Thursday

WEEK 25

19 Friday

20 Saturday

21 Sunday Summer Solstice
Father's Day, UK, Canada and USA

80. Mark of Léger-Fortuné-Alexandre Ricart. Gold, engraved and enamelled, set with an onyx cameo by Giovanni Carelli (1782–1834). France, Paris marks for 1809–19. Said to have been given by Napoleon to his sister Marie Annonciade Caroline, wife of Joachim Murat, created King of Naples in 1808. Murray Bequest

June

WEEK 26

22 Monday
New Moon

23 Tuesday

24 Wednesday

25 Thursday

26 Friday

27 Saturday

28 Sunday

Advertisement from *La Femme Chic* magazine. France, 1948

June · July

WEEK 27

29 Monday — *First Quarter*

30 Tuesday

1 Wednesday — Holiday, Canada (Canada Day)

2 Thursday

3 Friday — Holiday, USA (Independence Day)

4 Saturday — Independence Day, USA

5 Sunday

Breast ornament, 208 table-cut and faceted point-cut diamonds, set in gold, with enamel. Probably France, about 1620–30. Given by Dame Joan Evans

July

6 Monday

7 Tuesday   *Full Moon*

8 Wednesday

9 Thursday

WEEK 28

10 Friday

11 Saturday

12 Sunday

Locket, The Heneage or Armada Jewel. Enamelled gold, rock crystal, table-cut diamonds and Burmese rubies. Inside, miniature of Elizabeth I by Nicholas Hilliard (1537–1619) and enamelled Tudor rose inscribed in Latin 'Alas that so much virtue suffused with beauty should not last forever inviolate'. England, about 1595. Given by Lord Wakefield through the Art Fund

July

WEEK 29

13 Monday

Battle of the Boyne
Holiday, Northern Ireland

14 Tuesday

15 Wednesday

Last Quarter

16 Thursday

17 Friday

18 Saturday

19 Sunday

Photograph by Cecil Beaton (1904–80) of Princess Alexandra, The Honourable Lady Ogilvy. England, 1954

July

20 Monday

21 Tuesday

22 Wednesday *New Moon*

23 Thursday

WEEK 30

24 Friday

25 Saturday

26 Sunday

Brooch. Gold set with an emerald, turquoises and topazes. Unidentified maker's mark. France, Paris warranty mark for 1819–38

July · August

WEEK 31

27 Monday

28 Tuesday

First Quarter

29 Wednesday

30 Thursday

31 Friday

1 Saturday

2 Sunday

Detail of a necklet with pendant. Garnets set in silver. England, about 1760–80.
Given by Captain A. Heywood-Lonsdale

August

3 Monday   Summer Bank Holiday, Scotland
                       Holiday, Republic of Ireland

4 Tuesday

5 Wednesday

6 Thursday   Full Moon

WEEK 32

7 Friday

8 Saturday

9 Sunday

Pair of earclips and brooch. Boucheron. Gold and
platinum set with turquoises and diamonds.
France, about 1963.
The Bettine, Lady Abingdon Collection,
bequeathed by Mrs. T. R. P. Hole

August

WEEK 33

10 Monday

11 Tuesday

12 Wednesday

13 Thursday

Last Quarter

14 Friday

15 Saturday

16 Sunday

Advertisement from *La Femme Chic* magazine, France, 1948

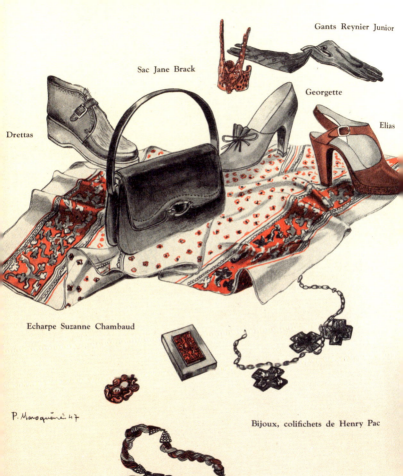

August

WEEK 34

17 Monday

18 Tuesday

19 Wednesday

20 Thursday   *New Moon*

21 Friday

22 Saturday   First Day of Ramadān (subject to sighting of the moon)

23 Sunday

Photograph by John French, Claire Bloom modelling white swan dress designed by John Cavanagh, *Woman's Own*, Britain, 1952

August

24 Monday

25 Tuesday

26 Wednesday

27 Thursday *First Quarter*

WEEK 35

28 Friday

29 Saturday

30 Sunday

Pendant (with reverse view). Enamelled gold openwork
set with sapphires, rubies, emeralds and rose-cut
diamonds, the back with painted enamel.
Western Europe, 1650–1700

August · September

WEEK 36

Summer Bank Holiday, UK exc. Scotland

31 Monday

1 Tuesday

2 Wednesday

3 Thursday

4 Friday *Full Moon*

5 Saturday

6 Sunday Father's Day, Australia and New Zealand

Necklace. Brilliant-cut rock crytals set in silver backed with gold. France, about 1790–1805. Given by Dame Joan Evans

September

7 Monday   Holiday, USA (Labor Day)
                                                                                              Holiday, Canada (Labour Day)

8 Tuesday

9 Wednesday

10 Thursday

WEEK 37

11 Friday

12 Saturday — Last Quarter

13 Sunday

Pendant. Made by Lucien Gautrait (1865–1937).
Gold, enamel, opals, diamonds and emeralds.
France, about 1900

September

WEEK 38

14 Monday

15 Tuesday

16 Wednesday

17 Thursday

18 Friday *New Moon*

19 Saturday *Jewish New Year (Rosh Hashanah)*

20 Sunday

Bracelet and tassel. Gold, coral and diamonds. Western Europe, about 1960.
The Bettine, Lady Abingdon Collection, bequeathed by Mrs. T.R.P. Hole

September

WEEK 39

Eid al Fitr, Ramadān ends
21 Monday

Autumnal Equinox
22 Tuesday

23 Wednesday

24 Thursday

25 Friday

First Quarter
26 Saturday

27 Sunday

Photograph by John French, Jean Shrimpton modelling jewellery, *Voice & Vision*, England, May 1963

September · October

28 Monday — Day of Atonement (Yom Kippur)

29 Tuesday — Michaelmas Day

30 Wednesday

1 Thursday

WEEK 40

2 Friday

3 Saturday — Festival of Tabernacles (Succoth), First Day

4 Sunday — Full Moon

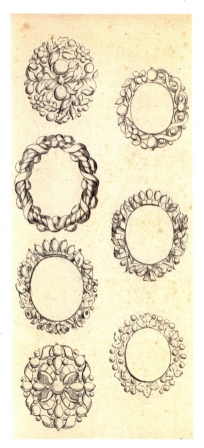

Traité des pierres précieuses et de la manière de les employer en parure. By Jean Henri Prosper (d.1769), Mlle Raimbau (fl.1762). Published in France, Paris, 1762

October

WEEK 41

5 Monday

6 Tuesday

7 Wednesday

8 Thursday

9 Friday

10 Saturday

Festival of Tabernacles (Succoth), Eighth Day

11 Sunday

Last Quarter

Maltese cross. Garnets set in gold. England, about 1800

October

12 Monday — Holiday, Canada (Thanksgiving)
Holiday, USA (Columbus Day)

13 Tuesday

14 Wednesday

15 Thursday

WEEK 42

16 Friday

17 Saturday

18 Sunday   *New Moon*

Brooch. Designed and made by George Hunt (1892–1960). Silver, gold, moonstones, sapphires and enamel. England, Birmingham, 1935
Bequeathed by Mrs. Ellen Amphlett

OCTOBER

WEEK 43

19 Monday

20 Tuesday

21 Wednesday

22 Thursday

23 Friday

24 Saturday   United Nations Day

25 Sunday   British Summer Time ends

Photograph by John French, Audrey White in feature "A Beauty loses her looks...",
Daily Express, 21 September 1950

OCTOBER · NOVEMBER

WEEK 44

26 Monday

First Quarter
Holiday, New Zealand (Labour Day)
Holiday, Republic of Ireland

27 Tuesday

28 Wednesday

29 Thursday

30 Friday

31 Saturday

Hallowe'en

1 Sunday

All Saints' Day

Bracelet in the form of a vine branch. Enamelled gold set with pearls. France, Paris, about 1850

November

2 Monday Full Moon

3 Tuesday

4 Wednesday

5 Thursday Guy Fawkes' Day

WEEK 45

6 Friday

7 Saturday

8 Sunday Remembrance Sunday, UK

Left: The Toilette, by Charles Robert Leslie (1794–1859).
Oil on panel. Britain, about 1849

Right: A Lady aged 29 in 1582. Formerly attributed to
Hermann Tom Ring (1520–97). Oil on oak panel.
Germany (possibly south), 1582

November

WEEK 46

9 Monday

Last Quarter

10 Tuesday

11 Wednesday

Holiday, USA (Veterans' Day)
Holiday, Canada (Remembrance Day)

12 Thursday

13 Friday

14 Saturday

15 Sunday

Pendant 'Winter Woodland'. Made by René Lalique. Enamel, glass and gold. France, about 1898.
Lent through the generosity of William and Judith Bollinger

November

16 Monday *New Moon*

17 Tuesday

18 Wednesday

19 Thursday

WEEK 47

20 Friday

21 Saturday

22 Sunday

Necklace. Designed by Sybil Dunlop (1889–1968). Silver, opals, rubies and stained chalcedony. England, London, about 1934

November

WEEK 48

23 Monday

24 Tuesday *First Quarter*

25 Wednesday

26 Thursday *Holiday, USA (Thanksgiving Day)*

27 Friday

28 Saturday

29 Sunday *First Sunday in Advent*

Brooch. Designed and made by Carrie Copson, a pupil of Arthur Gaskin. Silver, gold, mother of pearl and purple glass stones. England, Birmingham, about 1905. Given by Miss E. Copson

November · December

WEEK 49

30 Monday · St. Andrew's Day

1 Tuesday

2 Wednesday · Full Moon

3 Thursday

4 Friday

5 Saturday

6 Sunday

Advertisement from *La Femme Chic* magazine, France, 1948

December

7 Monday

8 Tuesday

9 Wednesday   Last Quarter

10 Thursday

WEEK 50

11 Friday

12 Saturday — Jewish Festival of Chanukah, First Day

13 Sunday

Left: Design for a pendant. Made by Arnold Lulls
(fl. 1584–1642). Pencil, pen and ink, watercolour,
bodycolour on paper. England, about 1550–60

Right: Design for an aigret. Made by Arnold Lulls
(fl. 1584–1642). Pencil, pen and ink, watercolour,
bodycolour on paper. England, about 1550–60

DECEMBER

WEEK 51

14 Monday

15 Tuesday

16 Wednesday   *New Moon*

17 Thursday

18 Friday   Islamic New Year (subject to sighting of the moon)

19 Saturday

20 Sunday

Photograph by John French, Jewellery, Harvey Nichols, *Vanity Fair*, England, July 1951

December

21 Monday   Winter Solstice

22 Tuesday

23 Wednesday

24 Thursday   *First Quarter*
Christmas Eve

WEEK 52

25 Friday

Christmas Day
Holiday, UK, Republic of Ireland, Canada, USA, Australia and New Zealand

26 Saturday

Boxing Day
(St. Stephen's Day)

27 Sunday

Dress ornaments, part of a set of forty-six. Made by Leopold Pfisterer. Commissioned by the Empress Catherine the Great (1729–96). Brilliant-cut diamonds set in silver. St Petersburg, Russia, 1764.
Cory Bequest

December · January

WEEK 1, 2010

28 Monday
Holiday, UK and Canada

29 Tuesday

30 Wednesday

31 Thursday
Full Moon
New Year's Eve

1 Friday
New Year's Day
Holiday, UK, Republic of Ireland, Canada,
USA and Australia

2 Saturday
Holiday, Scotland and New Zealand

3 Sunday

Photograph by John French, peony red velour coat with a white fleece lining by Brenner, cocktail dress in shot ribbed faille by Baker Sportswear, *Vanity Fair*, England, 1956

Notes